· DETERMINATI‖‖‖‖‖‖‖‖‖‖‖‖‖‖‖ T
P9-DVK-092
HIP · HOPE · PERSPECTIVE ·
OR NDS

A Special Gift

Presented to

Andy Brown

From

Dennis & Lori Munden

Date

H.S.
Graduation - 2004

IP · HOPE · PERSPECTIVE · G
NCIPLES · VICTORY · TEMPTA

Dear Graduate

LETTERS *of* WISDOM FROM

CHARLES R. SWINDOLL

Compiled and Edited by Terri Gibbs

All text originally appeared in *Living Above the
Level of Mediocrity* by Charles R. Swindoll.
© by Charles R. Swindoll 1987, 1989.

A J. Countryman Book

Designed by Koechel Peterson & Associates, Inc.,

ISBN: 0-8499-5495-9-SE
ISBN: 0-8499-5419-3

Printed and bound in the United States of America

CONTENTS

Foreword IV

Priorities 1

Ethics 5

Integrity 9

Flexibility 15

Optimism 19

Commitment 23

Creativity 29

Greatness 33

Dreams 37

Purpose 43

Mortality 47

Determination 53

Laughter 57

Generosity 61

Individuality 67

Godliness 71

Leadership 75

Hope 81

Perspective 85

Guidance 89

Accountability 93

Courage 97

Principles 103

Victory 107

Temptation 111

Friendships 117

Distinction 121

Contentment 125

Lifestyle 131

Excellence 135

*G*raduation marks an ending and a beginning. There are smiles, hugs, tears, shouts of joy, and caps sailing high into the air along with hopes and dreams. It is a time of celebration, excitement, and full-throttle enthusiasm.

Foreword

Great word, *enthusiasm*. Its Greek origin is *entheos*, "God in." It is the ability to see God in a situation that makes it exciting. Do you know that God is watching your life? Do you realize that? Something happens to us when we become convinced that God our heavenly Father is aware of and involved in our activities and is, in fact, applauding our lives.

Think of all you have accomplished to this point. Try to imagine the horizons and challenges of your future. As you mentally travel from the vanishing point of yesterday to the vanishing point of tomorrow you will find that God has been and always will be present. There is not a place in the entire scope of your existence where God is not there. There is purpose, there is meaning in the presence of God. Even in the things we may consider pointless, insignificant, trivial, or boring. Talk about an exciting thought!

Today may be the first day you realized that your heavenly Father is watching you in life. He is not absent, unconcerned, blind, deaf, or dead. He is watching because He cares. That can make all the difference in the world. Especially in a world where mediocrity calls the cadence ... where quality and integrity and authenticity are negotiables.

Call me a dreamer, but I'm convinced that achieving one's full potential is still a goal worth striving for—that excellence is still worth pursuing even if most yawn and a few sneer. While there may not be millions out there who think like this, there are still a few...a very important few. You are probably among them.

Therefore, as you graduate, I'd like to challenge you to follow God's best. More specifically, to live a "God-enthused" life. That's the purpose of these letters. They come from my heart to yours. I am excited for you, because I have unlimited expectations for your life—and, more importantly, unwavering faith in the One who can accomplish them.

Chuck Swindoll

Priorities

*L*ife is a lot like a coin;

you can spend it any way you wish,

but you can spend it only once.

Choosing one thing over

all the rest throughout life

is a difficult thing to do.

This is especially true when

the choices are so many and

the possibilities are so close.

To be completely truthful with you, however, we aren't left with numerous possibilities. Jesus Himself gave us the top priority:

"But seek first His kingdom and His righteousness; and all these things shall be added to you" (Matt. 6:33).

He said, in effect, "This is your priority; this comes first."

If I am to seek first in my life God's kingdom and God's righteousness, then whatever else I do ought to relate to that goal: where I work, with whom I spend my time, the one I marry, or the decision to remain single. Every decision I make ought to be filtered through the Matthew 6:33 filter: where I put my money, where and how I spend my time, what I buy, what I sell, what I give away.

Priorities

Living out the kingdom life means that everything must remain before the throne and under the authority of the ruler. Everything must be held loosely.

What tangibles are you holding onto? What are you gripping tightly? Have they become your security? Are you a slave to some image? Some name you're trying to live up to? Some job? Some possession? Some person? Let me give you a tip. If you cannot let it go, it's a priority to you. It is impossible to be a slave to things or people and at the same time be a faithful servant of God.

Life places before us hundreds of possibilities. Some are bad. Many are good. A few, the best. But each of us must decide, "What is my choice? What is my reason for living?" In other words, "What priority takes first place in my life?"

Ethics

We need heroes.

I mean genuine heroes,

authentic men and women

who are admired

for their achievements,

noble qualities, and courage.

Such people aren't afraid

to be different. They risk.

They stand a cut above.

Yet they are real human beings with flaws and failures like anyone else. But they inspire us to do better. We feel warm inside when we think about this rare breed of humanity. The kind we can look up to without the slightest suspicion of deception or hypocrisy. The kind who model excellence when no one is looking or for that matter when half the world is looking.

Ethics

I'm concerned that we seem to be running shy of folks like that. Certainly, there are some, but not nearly as many, it seems, as when I was a small boy. Back then I distinctly recall looking up to numerous people in various segments of society—politics, athletics, education, science, the military, music, religion, aviation—all of whom not only stood tall during their heyday, but they finished well. Society mourned their passing. This was no childhood fantasy, you understand; these were not make-believe matinee idols. I can still remember my dad being just as impressed as I was with certain folks—maybe more so. Some of our father-son conversations are still logged in my memory bank. And because he was inspired, so was I.

You may be surprised to know that for any number of people, you are the person others point to. It may be in the place where you work, and no one has even told you. It may happen where you live, and no neighbor has been brave enough to encourage you by saying, "You're the one everybody watches. You're very unique. We all respect you." It may be in your school where you are admired by colleagues and peers. If you knew how many felt that way, I'm convinced you would be all the more careful how you live.

I am certain of this—if you are one of those people, then you're not like the majority. You're living differently, and I commend you for it. It takes unusual people to make a difference in our world. Mediocre people impact no one, at least not for good. But one person of truth can impact the whole world!

Chuck Swindoll

Integrity

If some corporate position

is the god of your life, then something

terrible occurs within when it is

no longer a future possibility.

If your career, however, is simply

a part of God's plan and you keep it

in proper perspective, you can handle

a demotion just as well as

you can handle a promotion.

It all depends on who's first and what's first.

Breaking the magnet that draws things ahead of God is a lengthy and sometimes painful process.

There is a line found in the Jewish Talmud that puts it well: "Man is born with his hands clenched; he dies with them wide open. Entering life, he desires to grasp everything; leaving the world, all he possessed has slipped away."

Everything created was through Christ and His power, and furthermore, it was created for His honor. That includes everyday things today. If you have a good job, it's to be enjoyed for Him. If you have a nice salary, it's to be enjoyed and invested for Him. Do you have good health? It is for Him. Are you planning a move? It's to be for Him. You're thinking about a career change? It needs to be for Him. That is true because He's the ruler of our kingdom. He is Lord.

You're dating a young man. You think you're falling in love with this man. Does Christ have first place in that relationship? Or have you decided that a moral compromise really feels better? Maybe you have chosen not to maintain such a strict standard of purity as before. If you've made that priority decision, then face it—Christ really isn't in first place in that romance.

Integrity

Are you struggling right now between a decision that requires doing what is exactly right and losing closeness with an individual or giving in a little and keeping that friendship? You know the rest of the story. If Christ is going to have top priority, it must be according to the standard of His righteousness.

Just remember: Whatever is in first place, if it isn't Christ alone, it is in the wrong place.

Never take your cues
from the crowd.

Flexibility

*A*re you open to change?

People who make a difference

can be stretched, pulled,

pushed, and changed.

You heard it from me:

Traditionalism is an old dragon,

bad about squeezing the very life

out of its victims.

So never stop fighting it.

Let's be careful to identify the right opponent. It isn't tradition per se; it's traditionalism. I'm not trying to be petty, only accurate. The right kind of traditions give us deep roots—a solid network of reliable truth in a day when everything seems up for grabs. Among such traditions are those strong statements and principles that tie us to the mast of truth when storms of uncertainty create frightening waves of change driven by winds of doubt. For example: believing in the authority of holy Scripture, knowing and loving God, bowing to the Lordship of Jesus Christ, committing ourselves to others, and becoming people of genuine encouragement. Such traditions (there are others, of course) are valuable absolutes that keep us from feeling awash in a world of relativism and uncertainty.

Flexibility

However, there is a great deal of difference between tradition and traditionalism. By traditionalism, I have in mind mainly an attitude that resists change, adaptation, or alteration. It is holding fast to a custom or behavior that is being blindly and forcefully maintained. It is being suspicious of the new, the up-to-date, the different. It is finding one's security, even identity, in the familiar and therefore opposing whatever threatens that. And if you'll allow me one more, it is substituting a legalistic system for the freedom and freshness of the Spirit— being more concerned about keeping rigid, manmade rules than being flexible, open to creativity and innovation.

By now you've guessed where I stand. Clearly, my position is on the side of openness, allowing room for the untried, the unpredictable, the unexpected—all the while holding fast to the truth. Believe me, there are plenty of people around who feel it is their calling to tell others what to do and what to say. They are self-appointed wing-clippers who frown on new ways and put down high flight. They work hard to "squeeze you into their mold."

Whoever decides to soar must first fight through the flatland fog that hangs heavy over the swamp of sameness.

Chuck Swindoll

Optimism

Vision—the one essential

ingredient for being an original

in a day of copies gets lost,

overwhelmed by the odds.

Too bad! We start

focusing on the trouble.

Then we start comparing the odds.

The result is predictable: We become intimidated and wind up *defeated*.

What is your challenge? Which giants make you feel like a grasshopper when you face them? What does your future resemble when you measure it on the basis of facts and figures? You'd like not to surrender, right? You'd like to be courageous, wouldn't you? There is a way through, but you'll need one essential quality—*vision*.

Vision is the ability to see God's presence, to perceive God's power, to focus on God's plan in spite of the obstacles.

When you have vision it affects your attitude. Your attitude is optimistic rather than pessimistic. Your attitude stays positive rather than negative. Not foolishly positive, as though in fantasy, for you are reading God into your circumstances. So when a situation comes that cuts your feet out from under you, you don't throw up your arms and panic. You don't give up. Instead, you say, "Lord, this is Your moment. This is where You take charge. You're in this."

This is nothing more than having a strong belief in the power of God; having confidence in others around you who are in similar battles with you; and, yes, having confidence in yourself, by the grace

Optimism

of God. Refusing to give in to temptation, cynicism, and doubt. Not allowing yourself to become a jaded individual. Belief in oneself is terribly important.

Determination is hanging tough when the going gets rough. I have no magic wand to wave over your future and say, "All of a sudden everything is going to fall into place." Vision requires determination, a constant focus on God who is watching and smiling. Even in a world that is negative and hostile. Even in a world where the majority says, "We can't," you can. Trust God today. With eyes of faith, get back in the game. Play it with great enthusiasm!

Chuck Swindoll

People of excellence

are those who see through

the clutching greed of our times—

people who have declared

their undivided allegiance

to Christ's message, people who

have humbled themselves

to Christ's sovereign authority.

If you are greatly gifted, you may be able to do marvelous things that would cause the public to be swept up in your skills and in your abilities. In the process of your growing, you will find great temptation to make a name for yourself, to make a big splash, to gain attention, to get the glory, to strut around, to increase your fees, to demand your rights, and to expect kid–glove treatment. You're in authority now! People are talking about you!

Commitment

Let me remind you that if you're in life only for yourself, you'll have no endurance. On that precarious top of the ladder, you'll always have to maintain your balance by maneuvering and manipulating, lying, deceiving, and scheming. But if you're committed to kingdom–related excellence, when you go through times of testing, you can count on kingdom endurance to get you through.

If you're the kind of Christian who really wants the whole purpose of God, then you dare not leave out kingdom commitment. That means your motives must be investigated. For example, every time you make plans to acquire a sizable possession—a car, an expensive boat, a house, and such like—you must deal with it before God and ask: Is this His will? Would this honor Him? Would this glorify Him?

Am I suggesting that you take a vow of poverty? No, not that. My message is not that you go hungry and give up all nice things. I just say you give up control of them. Give all you have to the Lord God and trust Him to give back all that you need.

Chuck Swindoll

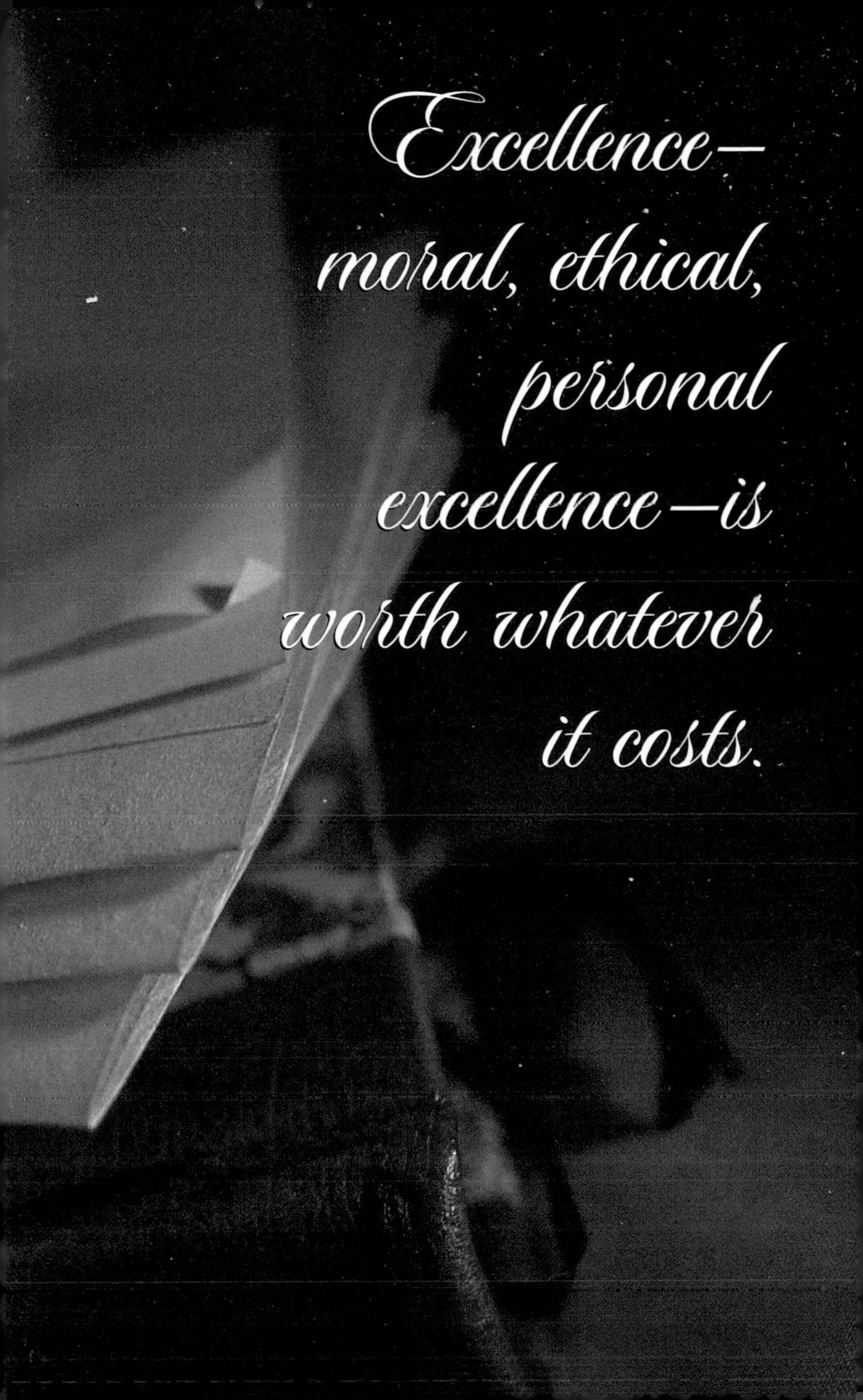

*Excellence—
moral, ethical,
personal
excellence—is
worth whatever
it costs.*

Creativity

God is a God of freshness and change.

But wait, before I leave that thought,

let me make something very clear:

God Himself isn't changing,

nor is His Son. He "is

the same yesterday and today,

yes and forever" (Heb. 13:8).

Isn't that a great thought?

God is no different this year than He was last year or a decade ago. Nor will He change one hundred years from now. But even though He is the same, His working is different. It stays fresh. His ways and methods are forever fresh, unpredictably new.

I need to warn you, if you like things to stay the same, you're going to be terribly uncomfortable in heaven. Everything is going to be new. God is a God of freshness and change. He flexes His methods. He alters His way so much, it's as if you've never seen it before. You can't imagine what it may be like next time.

God says we are to be "imitators" of Him, which really means we are to "mimic." Since God is a God of freshness and change, so we should be.

Creativity

If we are to fulfill this command, then I suggest that we stay fresh—that we remain open, innovative, willing to change.

Every age knows the temptation to try to restrict God's dealings. The majority of people in this world are maintainers. Once we get things set, we don't like them changed.

Are you open to change in your life? Are you willing to risk? Are you flexible enough to innovate? Are you willing to tolerate the sheer possibility of

making a massive change in your direction for life? "Lord, is it South America? Great! Or Indonesia? I'll do it. I'll move or change my profession. Fine! Are You leading me into a new venture? I'll do it. Count me in!"

That's the spirit! It may mean moving across the street. It may mean moving across the States. It may mean moving across the seas. How flexible are you? It may not involve a move at all, only a willingness.

Chuck Swindoll

Greatness

I'm sure it comes

as no surprise

to most of us

that we act out

precisely what we take in.

In other words,

we become what we think.

Long before that familiar line found its way into Psychology 101 and hyped-up sales meetings, the Bible included it in one of its ancient scrolls.

It just said it in a little different way: "For as he thinks within himself, so he is" (Prov. 23:7).

The secret of living a life of excellence is merely a matter of thinking thoughts of excellence. Really, it's a matter of programming our minds with the kind of information that will set us free. Free to be all God meant us to be. Free to soar! It will take awhile, and it may be painful—but what a metamorphosis!

Let me get to the heart of the issue. Since the mind holds the secrets of soaring, the enemy of our souls has made the human mind the bull's-eye

Greatness

of his target. His most insidious and strategic moves are made upon the mind. By affecting the way we think, he is able to keep our lives on a mediocre level.

Don't forget: Our minds were originally enemy-held territories. We were blinded by the power of the enemy. The mind was his "base of operations" until the light shone within. At that time, the veil was lifted and we were no longer blinded. It was a supernatural event in which new life was given, and the enemy was relieved of his command.

But I am increasingly more convinced that Satan doesn't want to give up his territory. He is a defeated foe who knows his future. Yet he fights to the last degree to maintain the hold he has had on us.

God is interested in our breaking free from such locks.

And what is God's ultimate goal?—To take "every thought captive." When He invades those lofty areas, His plan is to transform the old thoughts that defeat us into new thoughts that encourage us. He has to repattern our whole way of thinking. And He is engaged in doing that continually because old habits are so hard to break.

God's offer is nothing short of phenomenal! Remember it? It is "taking every thought captive to the obedience of Christ."

Chuck Swindoll

Dreams

There is an important dimension to hanging tough that you dare not miss. It is the thing that keeps you going. I call it a dream.

I don't mean those things we experience at night while we're asleep. No, by dream, I mean a God-given idea, plan, agenda, or goal that leads to God-honoring results.

Most of us don't dream enough. If someone were to ask you, "What are your dreams for this year? What are your hopes, your agenda? What are you trusting God for?" could you give a specific answer? I don't have in mind just occupational objectives or goals, although there's nothing wrong with those. But what about the kind of dreaming that results in character building, the kind that cultivates God's righteousness and God's rulership in your life?

Here are a few more ideas about dreams. Dreams are specific, not general. Dreams are personal, not public. God doesn't give anyone else my dreams on the online computer screen. He gives them to me personally. They're intimate images and ideas. Dreams can easily appear to others as extreme and illogical. If you share your dreams with the crowd, they'll probably laugh at you because you can't make logical sense out of them. Dreams are often accompanied by a strong desire to fulfill them. And they are always outside the realm of the expected. Sometimes they're downright shocking. They cause people to suck in their breath, to stand staring at you with their mouth open. A common response when you share a dream is, "You've gotta be kidding! Are you serious?"

Dreams

One more thought on dreams: This is the stuff of which leaders are made. If you don't dream, your leadership is seriously limited. To make things even more complicated, those who refuse to dream the impossible are always in the majority. Those who choose to live by sight will always outnumber those who live by faith.

So once you've decided to live differently, let God be your guide and hang tough—follow your dreams with determination.

Chuck Swindoll

People who soar are those who refuse to sit back and wish things would change.

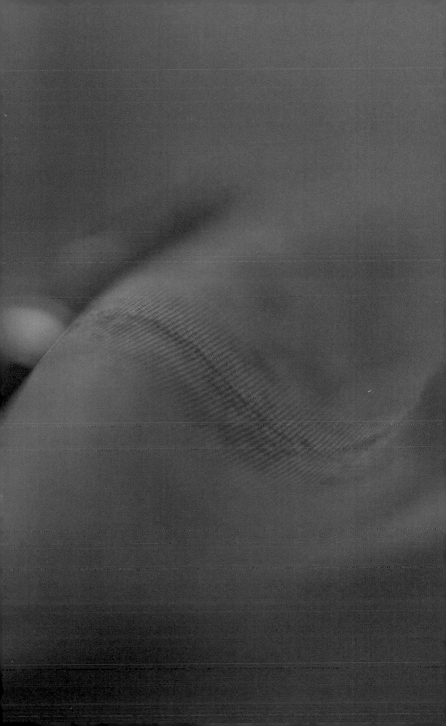

Purpose

*M*onotony and mediocrity

mesh like teeth in gears.

One spawns the other, leaving us

yawning, bored, and adrift.

In referring to monotony,

I do not have in mind

a lack of activity as much

as a lack of purpose.

We can be busy yet bored, involved yet indifferent. Life becomes tediously repetitious, dull, humdrum, pedestrian. In a word, blah.

Look into the faces of entertainers off the stage. Talk to physicians out of the office and hospital

Purpose

corridors. Those in the political arena are equally susceptible. Show me an individual who once soared, whose life was characterized by enthusiasm and excellence, but who no longer reaches those heights, and I'll show you a person who has probably become a victim of the blahs.

A blah attack may sound harmless, but it can leave us in an emotional heap, seriously questioning if life is worth it.

Yet even during your drab and seemingly meaningless assignments of life, God is there! He cares! He knows! From your yesterday to your tomorrow—God. From the little involvements to the big ones—God. From the beginning of school to the end of school—God. From the assignments that will never really make the headlines (which seems to be mere busy work) all the way to those things that gain international attention—God. He is there! So the very next time you feel those clammy, cold fingers of the blahs reaching around you, remember, "From yesterday until tomorrow, You, O Lord, are there. You care!"

Chuck Swindoll

Mortality

*L*ife is so short.

We really don't

have many years.

And to spend them

doing dumb stuff

seems like

such a waste.

I was intrigued several years ago when reading about some ghost towns littered across the plains of Nevada. The writer pointed out that there was every indication between the middle and the end of the 1800s that these towns would flourish forever. There were people by the thousands. There was gold in abundance. There were new buildings, vast plans, a spirit of excitement. There was wild

and woolly entertainment at every corner—houses and hotels, brothels and taverns, mines and money. The Gold Rush looked as if it would last forever. But suddenly; every-thing screeched to a halt. Almost overnight those bustling, loud pop-ulation centers became vacant dust collectors. The sound of the cash register ceased.

Today, except for a handful of eccentric desert dwellers, the stores and streets are empty. Those windswept ghost towns are now silent, hollow shells along forgotten sandy roads. Whatever happened to the boomtowns of Nevada?

What often looks as if it is here to stay and make a perpetual impact can be frighteningly temporary. When God says, "That's it; that's curtains," it's only a matter of time. It is the per-spective in all of this that holds us together. Our God is in complete control. He lets nothing out of

His grip. He starts one and stops another. He pushes one ahead and holds another back.

Yet our Lord is not some tyrannical God who stomps across heaven like the giant in Jack in the

Mortality

Beanstalk, swinging a club and waiting to give us a smashing blow to the head. No. Rather, it is as if He says to us, "You're Mine and I want you to walk in step with Me. I've arranged a plan so that walking with Me will result in a righteous lifestyle. If you make a decision not to walk with Me, I've also arranged consequences that will happen and you must live with them."

Yes, life is short. Yes, our sins are obvious; no one can deny that. But instead of thinking of these days as just about as futile as emptying waste-baskets, see the significance of them in light of God's plan. Ask him to help you view each day as He looks at it. He has a way of balancing out the good with the bad.

Chuck Swindoll

*Never quit
because someone
disagrees with you.*

Determination

When Jesus tells us to

"seek first the kingdom of God,"

the very word "seek" implies

a strong-minded pursuit.

J. B. Phillips paraphrases the idea

with "set your heart on."

The Amplified Bible says,

"Aim at and strive after."

The Greek text of Matthew's Gospel states a continual command: "Keep on continually seeking...." The thought is determination, which I define as "deciding to hang tough, regardless."

Determination

We need to keep in mind the difference between natural sight and supernatural vision. When we look at life with vision, we perceive events and circumstances with God's thoughts. And because His thoughts are higher and more profound than mere horizontal thinking, they have a way of softening the blows of calamity and giving us hope through tragedy and loss. It also enables us to handle times of prosperity and popularity with wisdom.

I'll be frank with you. I know of no more valuable technique in the pursuit of successful living than sheer, dogged determination. Nothing works in ministry better than persistence—persistence in godliness, determination to stay diligent in study, persistence in commitment to the priorities of ministry, determination in working with people. I often remind myself of those familiar words in 2 Timothy 4:1, "Preach the word; be ready in season and out of season." That's a nice way of saying, "Hang tough! Do it when it comes naturally and when it is hard to come by. Do it when you're up, do it when you're down. Do it when you feel like it, do it when you don't feel like it. Do it when it's hot, do it when it's cold. Keep on doing it. Don't give up."

That is persistence and determination. Staying at it. Hanging tough with dogged discipline. When you get whipped or when you win, the secret is staying at it.

Chuck Swindoll

Laughter

$\mathcal{I}$ know, I know—

"life is serious business."

If I hear that one more time,

I think I'll gag. I fully realize

that too much humor

can become offensive.

I recognize that it can be

taken to such an extreme

that it is inappropriate.

But doesn't it seem we have a long way to go before we are guilty of that problem? The final result of a joyless existence is sad—a superhigh-level intensity, borderline neurotic anxiety, an absence of just plain fun in one's work, a lack of relaxation, and the tendency to take ourselves much too seriously. We need to lighten up! Yes, spirituality and fun do go well together.

Scripture speaks directly to this issue, you know—especially the Proverbs:

A joyful heart makes a cheerful face, but when the heart is sad the spirit is broken (Prov. 15:13).

Amazing how that proverb goes right to the heart of the problem (no pun intended). We're not talking about a person's face here as much as we are about the heart. Internal joy goes public. We can't hide it. The face takes its cue from an inside signal.

A well-developed sense of humor reveals a well-balanced personality. Maladjusted people show a far greater tendency to miss the point in a funny remark. They take jokes personally. They take things that are meant to be enjoyable much too seriously. The ability to get a laugh out of everyday situations is a safety valve. It rids us of tensions and worries that could otherwise damage our health.

Laughter

You think I'm exaggerating the benefits? If so, maybe you've forgotten another proverb: "A joyful heart is good medicine, but a broken spirit dries up the bones" (Prov. 17:22). Isn't that eloquent? Literally, it says, "A joyful heart causes healing." What is it that brings healing to the emotions, healing to the soul? A joyful heart. And when the heart is right, a joyful countenance accompanies it!

Chuck Swindoll

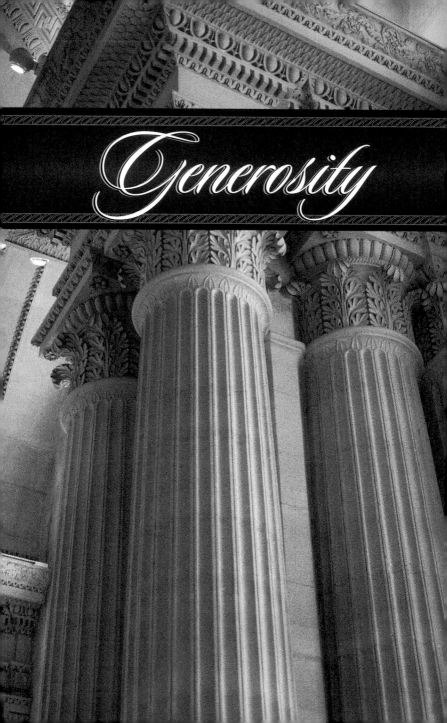

Reflect on God's

gifts to you.

In case you need

a little help,

read through

Psalm 103.

Bless the Lord, O my soul; and all that is within me, bless His holy name. Bless the Lord, O my soul, and forget none of His benefits; who pardons all your iniquities; who heals all your diseases; who redeems your life from the pit; who crowns you with lovingkindness and compassion; who satisfies your years with good things, so that your youth is renewed like the eagle. The Lord performs righteous deeds, and judgments for all who are oppressed (Ps. 103:1–6).

The psalmist lists several benefits to prod our thinking. As we reflect on God's gifts to us, it's helpful to be specific.

Do you have eyesight? It's a gift. Do you have a good mind? It's a gift. Do you have leadership abilities that cause others to follow? A good education? These are all gifts. Has He given you a

Generosity

family? Has He given you sufficient clothes? How about a nice, warm, soft bed at night or a comfortable place to live in the hot summer? Why, some even have more than one home! These are all gifts from God's hand. Reflect on His numerous gifts to you. It will increase your joy. And a smile will soon replace that frown.

Remind yourself of God's promises regarding generosity. God promises if you sow bountifully, you will reap bountifully. So give! Give abundantly! Even extravagant giving is honored by God. I've never known anyone who went bad because he or she was too generous. Remind yourself of His promises regarding generosity and start giving!

Don't be afraid of out-giving God. It is absolutely impossible to do that. He will keep every one of His promises related to generosity. Try Him!

Chuck Swindoll

Never use age as an excuse.

Individuality

*O*ne of the great American

myths is that we are all

a bunch of rugged individualists.

We would like to think that,

but it simply is not true.

There are some exceptions,

of course, but for the majority

it is not that way at all.

Deep within, we imagine ourselves as a mixture of Patrick Henry, Davy Crockett, John Wayne, and the prophet Daniel! But the truth of the matter is that most of us  would do anything to keep from being different. We'd much rather blend into the woodwork. One of our greatest fears is being ostracized, rejected by "the group." Ridicule is a pain too great for most to bear.

There are other fears—fear of being made to look foolish, fear of standing out in a crowd, fear of being talked about and misunderstood. Rather than rugged individualists, we are more like Gulliver of old, tied down and immobilized by tiny strands of fear, real or imagined. The result is both predictable and tragic: loss of courage.

Over thirty years ago I worked as a machinist in a shop where the vast majority were members of the local union. It didn't take me long to realize that the maintenance of a mediocre standard was one of the unwritten laws of that shop. Pressure was applied to anyone who worked unusually hard or produced more than the lower-than-average quota. Why? It made all the others look bad, and there was no way they would tolerate such a thing! Mild suggestions, if unheeded, would be followed by gentle nudges. Then, if still unheeded, the nudges would be followed by direct confrontation. If that was ignored, there were stronger measures taken to maintain the level of mediocrity. They would have no part of excellence. Conform or else!

Such pressure is not uncommon in numerous slices of life. The hard–charging high achiever at school is usually viewed with suspicion, not respect. Instead of others in the class picking up the pace and trying their best to do better, they would rather put down the student out front and make him or her look foolish. People don't want anyone to soar, especially if they prefer to slump!

Individuality

Chances are good that you feel the same pressure I'm illustrating. If not, color yourself fortunate. Few are the places today where eagle types pursuing excellence are admired and encouraged to reach greater heights.

Chuck Swindoll

Godliness

I need to be very candid with you. If you are a "Sunday Christian," you will not stand alone when outnumbered. Apart from a personal and vital faith in Jesus Christ, it is impossible to wage a winning effort against the system called "the world."

Trying to overcome the powerful magnet of the majority without help from above would be a frustrating and counterproductive effort. Only God can give us such transforming power through our faith in His Son.

Godliness

As far as God is concerned, a consistent godly life is well-pleasing, acceptable to Him. As far as you are concerned, it is an act of worship. It is a "spiritual service of worship."

We are like tiny islands of truth surrounded by a sea of paganism, but we launch our ship every day. We can't live or do business in this world without rubbing shoulders with those driven by the world's desires. God calls very few to be monks in a monastery. So we must make a practical decision not to be conformed while we are in the system, and at the same time, we must make a radical decision to give God the green light to transform our minds.

At the deepest level, even though the majority may not want to admit it, most people are conformists. That is why it is correctly termed a radical decision. Only a radically different mindset can equip folks like us to stand alone when we're outnumbered.

It takes courage to think alone, to resist alone, to stand alone—especially when the crowd seems so safe, so right. But remember God. Keep flying high like an eagle—far above the glue that snares the crowd. Up there it doesn't just seem safe and right, it is safe and right.

Leadership

$\mathcal{I}$f we hope to demonstrate

the level of excellence

modeled by Jesus Christ,

then we'll have to come to terms

with the kingdom we are

going to serve: the eternal kingdom

our Lord represented and told us

to seek (Matt. 6:23) or the

temporal kingdom of today.

Let's pause long enough to understand what I'm referring to when I mention the *kingdom*. It's one of those terms we like to use but seldom define.

Generally speaking, *God's kingdom is a synonym for God's rule.* Those who choose to live in His kingdom (though still very much alive on Planet Earth) choose to live under His authority.

For centuries God has been at work reestablishing His rulership. Jesus' words in Matthew describe the problem:

"No one can serve two masters; for either he will hate the one and love the other, or he will hold to one and despise the other. You cannot serve God and mammon. . . .

Leadership

"For all these things the Gentiles eagerly seek; for your heavenly Father knows that you need all these things. But seek first His kingdom and His righteousness; and all these things shall be added to you" (6:24, 32–33).

All this leads me to some helpful news, some bad news, and some good news! The kingdom is the invisible realm where God rules as supreme authority. That's *helpful news*. The *bad news* is that we, by nature, don't want Him to rule over us; we much prefer to please ourselves. We don't want anybody other than our-selves ruling over us! Much like those people in a story Jesus once told, "We do not want this man to reign over us!" (Luke 19:14).

Now, the *good news*. We don't have to live that way. God has given us an avenue of escape. It's called a birth from above. And not until we experience a spiritual rebirth will we submit to God's rule.

So when I write of God's kingdom, I'm referring to His rightful authority over our lives. I remind you—only by letting Him reign in your life can you experience true excellence.

Chuck Swindoll

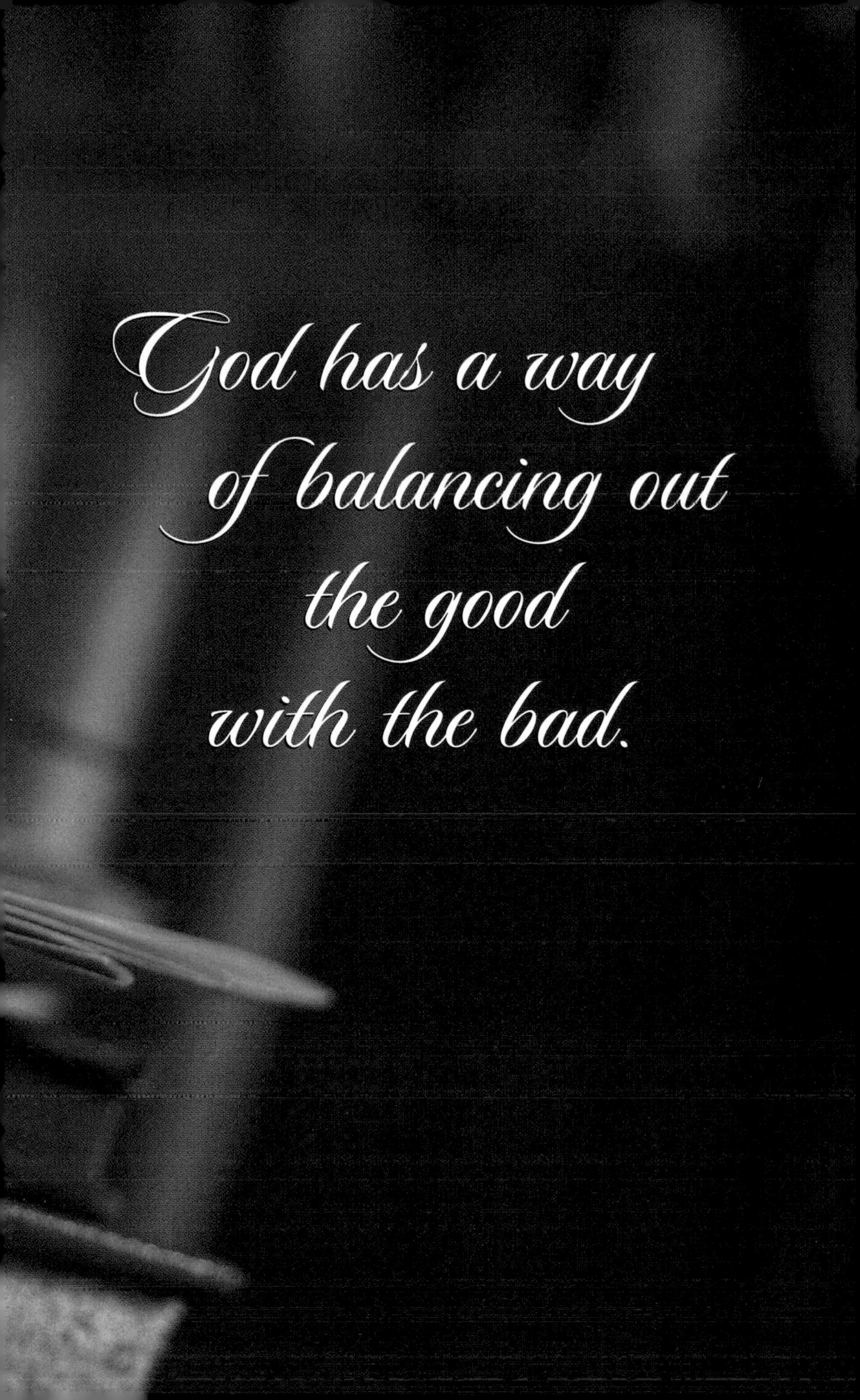

God has a way
of balancing out
the good
with the bad.

Hope

Can you remember

a recent "gray slush" day?

Of course you can. So can I.

The laws of fairness and justice

were displaced by

a couple of Murphy's Laws.

Your dream dissolved into a nightmare. High hopes took a hike. Good intentions got lost in a comedy of errors, only this time nobody was laughing. You didn't soar, you slumped. Instead of "pressing on the upward way," you felt like telling Bunyan to move over as you slid down into his Slough of Despond near Doubting Castle, whose owner was Giant Despair. Discouragement is just plain *awful*.

One of the greatest benefits to be gleaned from the Bible is perspective. When we get discouraged, we temporarily lose our perspective.

Little things become mammoth. A slight irritation, such as a pebble in a shoe, seems huge. Motivation is drained away and, worst of all, hope departs.

God's Word is tailor-made for gray-slush days. It sends a beam of light through the fog. It signals safety when we fear we'll never make it through. Such big-picture perspective gives us a hope transplant, and within a brief period of time, we have escaped the bleak and boring and we're back at soaring.

God has an ultimate goal in mind: that we might have hope. And what leads to such a goal?

Two things: perseverance and encouragement from the Scriptures. Again, the goal is hope. God has not designed a life of despondency for us. He wants His people to have hope. And He says such hope comes from the teaching of the Old Testament. Through endurance and through encouragement from the Scriptures, we can gain hope.

Hope

He promises us hope—relief from discouragement. Yes, it's available. And we can actually stand firm through discouraging times but only if we apply His instructions. Hard as it may be for you to believe, you will be able to walk right through those "gray slush" days with confidence. The One who gives perseverance and encouragement will escort you through the down days, never leaving you in the lurch.

Discouragement may be awful, but it is not terminal.

Chuck Swindoll

Perspective

*A*lmost every week

I come into contact

with people who have

been misled, thinking

that success depends

solely upon talent or

brilliance or education.

But the list doesn't end there. For some it's getting the breaks, pulling the right strings, having the right personality, being in the right place at the right time, knowing the right people, playing their cards right.

You see, it is our natural tendency to focus on the external, to be overly impressed with that which is seen. Wouldn't it be wonderful to develop the ability to look at a heart? Wouldn't it be great to be free of the limitations of strictly physical sight so that we could read hidden character traits?

Frankly, I think those who are physically blind often see more than those of us who are sighted. They often perceive much more than we can in the tone of a voice or in the sound of approaching

Perspective

footsteps or in the grip of a handshake. But we who have sight usually lack this insightful depth perception; the ability to detect the deeper things, the unspoken, the character, the hidden condition of the unspoken. And although God is able (and willing) to give us this ability, it isn't something we're born with. I'd like to make three significant observations.

First: Age has little to do with achievement and nothing to do with commitment.

Second: A godly walk is basic to a positive life.

Third: Convictions are a matter of choice, not force.

We must keep on continually pursuing—seeking to see life from the heart.

Chuck Swindoll

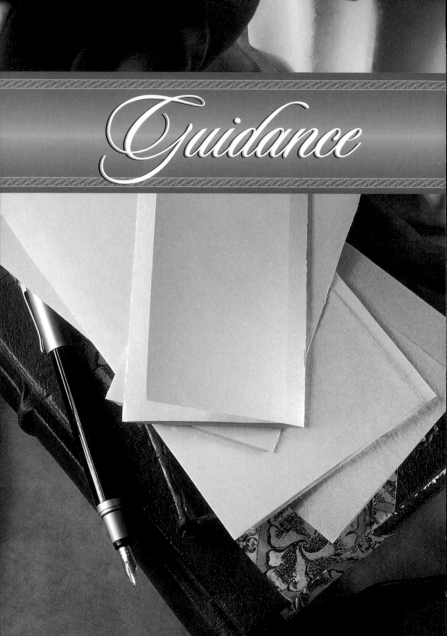

Guidance

God offers instruction,

but then it's our move.

We must accept His instruction

and apply it to our lives.

Then, and only then,

can we expect to cash in on

the benefits of His instruction.

So you see, application is the

essential link between

instruction and change.

Imagine, if you will, that you work for a company whose president found it necessary to travel out of the country and spend an extended period of time abroad. So he says to you and the other trusted employees, "Look, I'm going to leave. And while I'm gone, I want you to pay close attention to the business. You manage things while I'm away. I will write you regularly. When I do, I will instruct you in what you should do from now until I return from this trip." Everyone agrees. He leaves and stays gone for a couple of years. During that time he writes often, communicating

 his desires and concerns. Finally he returns. He walks up to the front door of the company and immediately discovers everything is in a mess—weeds flourishing in the flower beds, windows broken across the front of the building, the gal at the front desk dozing, loud music roaring from several offices, two or three people engaged in horseplay in the back room. Instead of making a profit, the business has suffered a great loss. Without hesitation he calls everyone together and with a frown asks, "What happened? Didn't you get my

letters?" You say, "Oh, yeah, sure. We got all your letters. We've even bound them in a book. And some of us have memorized them. In fact, we have 'letter study' every Sunday. You know, those were really great letters." I think the president would then

Guidance

ask, "But what did you do about my instructions?" And, no doubt, the employees would respond, "Do? Well, nothing. But we read every one!"

In the very same way, God has sent us His instruction. He has preserved every word of it in a Book, the Bible. It's all there, just as He communicated it to us. When He returns for His own, He is not going to ask us how much we memorized or how often we met for study. No, He will want to know, "What did you do about my instructions?"

Chuck Swindoll

Accountability

*W*hat do we mean

by accountability?

In the simplest terms,

it is answering the hard questions.

Accountability includes opening

one's life to a few carefully selected,

trusted, loyal confidants

who speak the truth—

who have the right to examine, to question, to appraise, and to give counsel.

People who are accountable usually have four qualities:

Vulnerability—capable of being wounded, shown to be wrong, even admitting it before being confronted.

Teachability—a willingness to learn, being quick to hear and respond to reproof, being open to counsel.

Availability—accessible, touchable, able to be interrupted.

Honesty—committed to the truth regardless of how much it hurts, a willingness to admit the truth no matter how difficult or humiliating the admission may be. Hating all that is phony or false.

Accountability

That's a tough list! As I look back over those four qualities, I am more than ever aware of why accountability is resisted by the majority. Those with fragile egos can't handle it. And prima donna types won't tolerate it. They have a greater desire to look good and make a stunning impression than anything else. I mean, "the very idea of someone probing into my life!"

Don't misunderstand. I'm not suggesting for a moment that accountability gives the general public carte blanche access to any and all areas of one's private life. If you will glance back a few lines you will notice I referred to "a few carefully selected, trusted, loyal confidants.'" They are the ones who have earned the right to come alongside and, when it seems appro-priate and necessary, ask the hard questions, to serve in an advisory capacity, bringing perspective and wisdom where such may be lacking.

In our society, where privacy is a reward of promotion and a life of virtual secrecy is the pre-rogative of most leaders, a lack of accountability is considered the norm. This is true despite the fact that unaccountability is both unwise and unbiblical, not to mention downright perilous!

Today we need others to hold us accountable. Sometimes an objective opinion will reveal a blind spot. Sometimes we may simply need a sounding board to help keep us on target. Just remember—not one of us is an island. We need one another.

Chuck Swindoll

Courage

Someone once wrote,

"Sow a thought, reap an act.

Sow an act, reap a habit.

Sow a habit, reap your character.

Sow your character, reap your destiny."

Standing tall when tested takes courage—constant, relentless, never-give-up courage! You can be sure that the old flesh will fight for its arousal and satisfaction. All it takes is a little rationalization—just a little. Just look the other way. Just shrug it off. Don't sweat it. And before long you have a rattlesnake in your sleeping bag.

Courage

First: *Standing tall starts with the way we think.* It has to do with the *mind.* As I've said so often, being a person of inner strength is really a mental factor. It has to do with the way we think about God, ourselves, and others. Then it grows into the way we think about business, the way we think about dating, the way we think about marriage and the family, the way we think about the system that is designed to destroy faith and bring us down to a lower standard.

Second: *Standing tall calls for strong discipline.* This has to do with the *will.* Disciplining the eyes, the ears, the hands, the feet. Keeping moral tabs on ourselves, refusing to let down the standards. People of strength know how to turn right thinking into action—even when insistent feelings don't agree.

Third: *Standing tall limits your choice of personal friends*. This has to do with *relationships*. What appears harmless can prove to be dangerous. Perhaps this is as important as the other two factors combined. Cultivate wrong friendships and you're a goner. This is why we are warned not to be deceived regarding the danger of wrong associations. Without realizing it, we could be playing with fire.

Sow the wind and, for sure, you'll reap the whirl-wind. Eagles may be strong birds, but when the wind velocity gets fierce enough, it takes an enormous amount of strength to survive. Only the ultrapowerful can make it through the whirlwind.

It takes courage to think alone,
to resist alone, to stand alone—
especially when the crowd
seems so safe, so right.

Principles

I think we need to sign

a mental declaration of independence.

Let's put our name on the line,

pledging ourselves with firm resolve,

much like those brave men did

on July 4, 1776, in Philadelphia

when they signed the

Declaration of Independence.

Did you know that of the fifty-six courageous men who signed that original document in Philadelphia, many did not survive the war that followed? Five were captured by the British and tortured before they died. Nine others died in the Revolutionary War, either from its hardships or its bullets. Twelve had their homes sacked, looted, burned, or occupied by the enemy. Two lost their sons in battle. One had two sons captured. Yes, the price of freedom was high indeed for those men. But deciding to be free, to think and live independently, to soar above the masses is always a costly decision.

In today's vernacular, committed individuals live with shallow tent pegs. They may own things, but nothing owns them. They have come to terms with merchandise that has a price tag and opted for commitment to values that are priceless.

Denying oneself is not to be equated with losing one's uniqueness or becoming of no value. There have been great people in each generation who modeled self-denial as they made significant contributions to humankind.

Principles

For years I taught that we are to "count the cost." It seemed so plausible. But suddenly one day, it dawned on me that Jesus never once told His followers to count the cost. No—He's the One who has already done that. He is the King who has already determined what it will take to encounter and triumph over life's enemies. And what will it take? A few strong, quality-minded champions whose commitment is solid as stone. And the cost will be great.

*P*icture for a moment

the barrenness and

bleakness that happens in

a life when compromise occurs.

It doesn't come immediately.

At first it's fun to run

with the wrong crowd.

There's some zip, a little excitement; there's a measure of thrill and pizzazz in being a part of the in-group. But inevitably the fleshly investment starts to yield its carnal dividends. And when that happens you suffer as you've never suffered before.

Victory

Perhaps the words "very low" paint a picture of bleakness that describes you at this very moment. You have ignored God's warnings and pushed your strong convictions aside as you associated with the wrong crowd. But now you are at the end of your rope. You're discouraged. You have failed miserably. You're thinking, What a terrible way to live!

All of us have spent time in that miserable camp called Reaping What Was Sown. En route, there's enough pleasure to make it seem like fun, but when it's all said and done, it's downright awful. There is no discouragement like the discouragement that comes from self-generated wrongdoing. Enduring the consequences of one's own irresponsibility creates feelings of grief and discouragement that defy description.

That's enough about the problem. What we really need are specific suggestions that get us back on track. First, you need to openly acknowledge what caused your condition. Openly admit that you have failed to stand alone as a true child of God. You see, you weren't built to live that way. You have allowed someone else to call your cadence. You're marching out of step with your Instructor. And the Lord speaks directly: "You have not obeyed Me."

Second, focus directly on the Lord, not on the odds against you. Everything depends on where your focus is. You must discipline yourself to focus directly on the Lord, not on those odds!

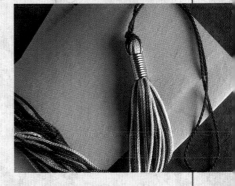

Get this straight and never forget it: You will not stand alone when outnumbered or stand tall when tested or stand firm when discouraged if your focus remains on the odds. Your eyes must be trained on the Lord.

Chuck Swindoll

Temptation

May I remind you of four

of the more powerful perils

that can level even the mightiest?

They are fortune, fame,

power, and pleasure.

Each works overtime

to win a hearing,

to gain a foothold,

to woo us in.

Whether subliminal, subtle, strong, or supreme, these messages search for chinks in our armor as they appeal to our natural appetites. "Get rich!" (fortune). "Become known!" (fame). "Gain control!" (power). "Be satisfied!" (pleasure). Each of these attractive snares invites our attention, holds out a juicy carrot, makes beautiful promises; yet each is an enemy always crouching and ready to plunge. Being masters of deceit, these messages employ one favorite method throughout our lives—*temptation.*

Let me mention a very practical thing about temptation. I have found that if I can stop the process fairly early, I'm safe. But if I leave my hiding place and venture toward the bait, there is

Temptation

a point of no return. I cannot turn around. If I go that far, I'm sunk.

So how can we have victory over temptation? First, *our natural focus must be counteracted.* Openly confess your weakness. Hide nothing. Use Scripture memory to replace sensual thoughts with spiritual thoughts.

Second, *our leisure time must be guarded.* Cultivate a plan, perhaps an exercise program, an intensive reading program, a hobby, a series of practical projects to occupy your time. Watch out for those video movies! If necessary, keep the television off. And stay away from the magazine rack.

Third, *our close companions must be screened.* Take a good look at your circle of friends. Do an honest evaluation of those with whom you spend personal time. I can offer you a principle you can bank on: Until you clean up your companionships, you'll never clean up your life.

Fourth, *our vow to God must be upheld.* Just as jealously as we would guard the marriage vows, we're to guard our promises to God and our commitment to purity.

Excellence—moral, ethical, personal excellence—is worth whatever it costs. Pay the price. Start today! Nothing less will ever satisfy you or glorify God.

Chuck Swindoll

Even in a world where the majority says, "We can't," you can.

Friendships

The world in which
one person lives is too
limited and restricted.
When rubbing shoulders
with another, we gain
a panoramic view,
which allows us
to see the whole picture.

"As in water face reflects face, so the heart of man reflects man" (Prov. 27: 19). That's so picturesque! People provide a clear reflection of what is in the heart. A mirror goes only skin deep. The counsel of a friend reflects what is down inside.

I'm talking about people who love you too much to let you play in dangerous traffic. They also love you too much to let you start believing in your own stuff. When they spot conceit rearing its head, they say so. But they also love you too much to let you be too hard on yourself. Like Jonathan with David, they are messengers of great encouragement.

"He who walks with wise men will be wise, but the companion of fools will suffer harm" (Prov. 13:20). That statement is not a verse written to teenagers in high school, though it certainly would apply. I clearly remember my high school years, don't you? Many of us ran around with others who were tougher than we, so we could cover up our own feelings of inadequacy. My mother kept saying to me, "Charles, every time you run with the wrong crowd, you do wrong. When you are with the right crowd, you do right." Her counsel is still true. If I were to run with the wrong crowd, I would be tempted to do wrong.

And it doesn't stop when we turn twenty. It goes on into adult years as well. If you choose a wrong set of co-workers, you'll practice wrong things in your business. If you choose a wrong set of friends, you'll practice wrong things in your social life. Run with those who do drugs, and you'll wind up doing the same.

Friendships

But—the flip side—those who walk with the wise learn from them. You need someone who will say, "I'm not sure how healthy that is. I'm glad you asked me. Let's talk about it." And that person will help point out the traps you could fall into if you kept tracking in that direction.

Other eyes, more perceptive and objective than ours, can see traps that we may fail to detect.

Chuck Swindoll

Distinction

The essential question
isn't difficult to state:
How can I, a person who has
absorbed so many years
of mediocre thinking, change?
How can I, like a caterpillar,
move from squirming in the dirt
to enjoying the sweet nectar
in God's creation?

As in the caterpillar's case, a radical metamorphosis must occur. It is a process that will be difficult, demanding, and lengthy—but, oh, how sweet the results! If you are really serious about conquering mediocrity (which, remember, starts in the mind), then I have three words to offer—memorize, personalize, and analyze.

Distinction

Memorize. In order for old defeating thoughts to be invaded, conquered, and replaced by new, victorious ones, a process of reconstruction must transpire. The best place I know to begin this process of mental cleansing is with the all important discipline of memorizing Scripture. I realize it doesn't sound very sophisticated or intellectual, but God's Book is full of powerful ammunition! And dislodging negative and demoralizing thoughts requires aggressive action. I sometimes refer to it as a mental assault.

Personalize. Here's where the excitement intensifies. As you begin the process of replacing old, negative thoughts with new and encouraging ones, put yourself into the pages of the Bible. Use I, me, my, mine as you come across meaningful statements.

Analyze. Instead of continuing to tell yourself you are little more than a helpless victim, take charge! As soon as you catch yourself responding negatively or defensively, think—analyze the situation. Then ask yourself a few tough questions. "Why am I getting so hot and bothered by this?" Or "Is there something I'm afraid of?" Or, maybe, "Am I reacting negatively because I have a reason or simply because I've formed some bad habits?"

Maybe the challenge to memorize, personalize, and analyze seems too simplistic to you. Perhaps you expected something else. You really expected some high-powered "secret" to success. No, I have no quick 'n' easy secret, no overnight-success pill you can take. Perhaps the best single-word picture is *visualize*. Mentally visualize being  on a higher plane. Then once you "see it," begin to believe it and behave like it!

Chuck Swindoll

Contentment

Let's take a brief look at greed.

Practically speaking, greed is

an inordinate desire for more,

an excessive, unsatisfied hunger

to possess. Like an untamed beast,

greed grasps, claws, reaches,

clutches, and clings—

stubbornly refusing

to surrender.

The word *enough* is not in this beast's vocabulary. Akin to envy and jealousy, greed is nevertheless distinct. Envy wants to have what someone else possesses. Jealousy wants to possess what it already has. But greed is different. Greed is forever discontented and therefore insatiably craving, longing, wanting, striving for more, more, more.

The Greeks had a curious word they used when referring to greed. The word means "a thirst for having more." To illustrate, it's probably fanciful yet fairly descriptive to think of a fellow who is thirsty taking a drink of salt water, which only makes him thirstier. His thirst causes him to drink even more, which ultimately results in making him terribly sick. And if he continues to drink he could die.

Contentment

That's the whole point of greed. You'll want more and more of something that really isn't good for you. And in the getting of it, you'll suffer the painful consequences. That is why Jesus warns, "Beware. Be on your guard. This thing is like a cancer—an insatiable leech that will suck the life right out of you." Enough will never be enough.

Life does not—cannot—revolve around things if one hopes to achieve true excellence.

There's nothing in the world wrong with making a nice living. Nor is there anything wrong with being eminently wealthy if you earn and handle it correctly. But there's something drastically wrong when you keep it all to yourself! God gave it to you so you could, in turn, give it back to Him, to others—yes, in abundance. The only reason I can imagine for God's allowing anyone to make more than one needs is to be able to give more. We certainly can't take it with us, that's for sure!

Chuck Swindoll

*God deserves
our very best;
nothing more,
nothing less,
nothing else.*

Lifestyle

*W*e live in a negative,

hostile world. Face it, my friend,

the system that surrounds us

focuses on the negatives:

what is wrong, not what is right;

what is missing, not what is present;

what is ugly, not what is beautiful;

what is destructive, not what is constructive; what cannot be done, not what can be done; what hurts, not what helps; what we lack, not what we have. You question that? Pick up your local newspaper and read it through. See if the majority of the news doesn't concern itself (and the reader) with the negatives. It's contagious!

This negative mindset leads to incredible feelings of anxiety. Surround most people with enough negatives and I can guarantee the result: fear, resentment, and anger. Negative information plus hostile thinking equals anxiety.

We are also engulfed in mediocrity and cynicism (a direct result of living in a negative world). Without the motivation of divinely empowered insight and enthusiasm, people tend toward the "average," doing just enough to get by. Thus, the fallout from the system is mediocrity. The majority dictates the rules, and excitement is replaced with a shrug of the shoulders. Excellence is not only lost in the shuffle, whenever it rears its head, it is considered a threat.

That's why most people choose not to live differently. Those who take their cues from the system blend into the drab backdrop of the majority. Words like "Just go with the flow" and "Don't make waves" and "Who cares?" begin to gain a hearing.

Stop and think. In a world where all that cynicism is present, what is absent? Courage! That strong muscle of character that gives a nation its

Lifestyle

pride and gives a person the will to excel is gone.

I challenge you to be different, to stand apart from the crowd, with inner fortitude and strength of character—be disciplined to remain consistent, strong, and diligent regardless of the odds or the demands. Have courage!

Excellence

*M*ediocrity is fast becoming
the by-word of our times.
Every imaginable excuse is now
used to make it acceptable,
hopefully preferred. Budget cuts,
time deadlines, majority opinion,
and hard-nosed practicality are
outshouting and outrunning excellence.

Those forces seem to be winning the race. Incompetence and status quo averages are held up as all we can now expect, and the tragedy is that more and more people have virtually agreed. Why worry over the small stuff? Why bother with the genuine now that the artificial looks so real? If the public buys it, why sweat it?

To make it painfully plain, why think clearly since most folks want someone else to think for them? Why live differently in a society where it's so much easier to look the same and swim down-stream? Why fight fiercely when so few seem to care? Why stand courageously if it means risking ridicule, misunderstanding, or being considered a dreamer by some and a fool by others?

Why, indeed? To quote young David just before he took on that Philistine behemoth in the Valley of Elah, "Is there not a cause?" Must we wait for someone else to establish our standard or to set our pace? Not on your life! It is my firm conviction that those who impact and reshape the world are the ones committed to living above the level of mediocrity. There are still too many opportunities for excellence, too much demand for distinctiveness, to be satisfied with just getting by.

Excellence is a difficult concept to communicate because it can easily be misread as neurotic perfectionism or snooty sophistication. But it is neither. On the contrary, it is the stuff of which greatness is made. It is the difference between just getting by and soaring—that which sets apart the significant from the superficial, the lasting from the temporary.

A commitment to excellence is neither popular nor easy. But it is essential. Excellence in integrity and morality as well as ethics and scholarship. Excellence in physical fitness and spiritual fervor just as much as excellence in relationships and craftsmanship.

Since it is the living Lord in the final analysis who appraises our excellence, it is He whom we must please and serve, honor and adore.

Chuck Swindoll

P.S. It lies before you now. . .

the untrod path,

the unopened door,

the mountain peak,

the broad, blue heavens.

I challenge you. Walk that path,

open that door, climb the

mountain heights. The sky's the limit.

Let God be your guide

and hang tough—follow your

dreams with determination.

And when you find yourself

inundated with choices, don't be afraid.

Be wise. Choose God's way—

choose excellence.

My prayers are with you.

REAMS · PURPOSE · MORTAL

DUALITY · GODLINESS · LEAD

Y · COURAGE · PRINCIPLES · V

MENT · LIFESTYLE · EXCELLE

OMMITMENT · CREATIVITY

NATION · LAUGHTER · GENE

PERSPECTIVE · GUIDANCE ·

TATION · FRIENDSHIPS · DISTI

RITIES · ETHICS · INTEGRITY

GREATNESS · DREAMS · PUR

ROSITY · INDIVIDUALITY · GO

COUNTABILITY · COURAGE ·

TION · CONTENTMENT · LIFE

TY · FLEXIBILITY · OPTIMISM

· PURPOSE · MORTALITY · D

UALITY · GODLINESS · LEADE

COUNTABILITY · COURAGE ·